PLA

by Julia Grogan

SAMUEL FRENCH

FOR AMATEUR PRODUCTION ENQUIRIES

UNITED KINGDOM AND WORLD
EXCLUDING NORTH AMERICA
licensing@concordtheatricals.co.uk
020-7054-7298

Each title is subject to availability from Concord Theatricals, depending upon country of performance.

USE OF COPYRIGHTED MUSIC

USE OF COPYRIGHTED THIRD-PARTY MATERIALS

IMPORTANT BILLING AND CREDIT REQUIREMENTS

PLAYFIGHT was first produced by Grace Dickson Productions and Theatre Uncut at Paines Plough's Roundabout at Summerhall, as part of Edinburgh Festival Fringe 2024. The cast was as follows:

ZAINAB . . . . .Nina Cassells
KEIRA . . . . Sophie Cox
LUCY . . . . Lucy Mangan

Writer – Julia Grogan
Director – Emma Callander
Designer – Hazel Low
Composer & Sound Designer – Roly Botha
Lighting Designer – Kate Bonney
Movement Director & Choreographer – Aline David
Production Manager – Adam Jefferys
Stage Manager – Iona Hicks
Producer – Grace Dickson
Associate Producer for GDP – Rory Thomas Howes

Playfight was written by Julia Grogan and is her debut play. *Playfight* won The Experienced Theatre Practitioners Early Playwriting Award in 2020. In 2021, the play went on to be shortlisted for the Papatango New Writing Prize, the Theatre Uncut Political Playwriting Award and the Women's Prize for Playwriting. The play is currently a co-production between Grace Dickson Productions and Theatre Uncut, in association with Bristol Old Vic.

CAST

NINA CASSELLS | Zainab
Nina graduated from Guildhall School of Music and Drama in 2024, where she was the recipient of the Laurence Olivier Bursary. Theatre includes: *Swive* (The Globe, dir. Natalie Abrahami), *The Crucible* (The Yard, dir. Jay Miller). Radio includes: *Oliver: London to Lagos* (BBC Radio 4, dir. Michael Buffong). Theatre while training includes: *Yerma* (dir. Sophie Dillon Moniram), *The Trojan Women* (dir. Patsy Rodenburg), *The Seagull* (dir. Lyndsey Turner).

SOPHIE COX | Keira
Sophie recently graduated from Guildhall School of Music and Drama. *Playfight* marks Sophie's professional debut. Theatre whilst training includes: *Jane Eyre, Comedy of Errors, Days of Significance* (Guildhall).

LUCY MANGAN | Lucy
Training: The Royal Central School of Speech & Drama. Theatre includes: *Macbeth* (Wessex Grove UK/US Tour); *Harry Potter And The Cursed Child* (Palace Theatre); *Living Newspaper* (Royal Court); *Queen Margaret* (The Royal Exchange); *Let The Right One In* (National Theatre of Scotland); *Danger Brigade* (Crybabies Comedy); *Trip* (Stockwell Playhouse); *Before I Was A Bear* (CentrE17); *Alice In The Cuckoo's Nest* (Librarian Theatre); *Moonface* (Guttersnipe Theatre) Television includes: *The Great, Doctors*. Film includes: *The Magic Finger, Disconnected*. Radio includes: *The Christchurch Murder, Vampirella, INK 2 minute plays*.

CREATIVE TEAM

JULIA GROGAN | Writer
Julia trained as an actor at Rose Bruford College, graduating in 2018. She joined the Royal Court Writers' Group and went on to write her debut play, *Playfight*. The play won the ETPEP Playwriting Award, Papatango Award, the Theatre Uncut Award and the Women's Prize for Playwriting. Julia co-wrote and starred in dark historical-comedy *Belly Up* which premiered at VAULT Festival 2020 and went onto sell-out, five-star run at The Turbine Theatre in 2021. The production is in development with the RSC. Her theatre company, Dirty Hare's show, *Gunter* premiered at Edinburgh Fringe 2023, and received five stars, a Scotsman Fringe First and placed her as one of The Stage's five break out theatre makers. *Gunter* transferred to the Royal Court Theatre in April 2024. Julia currently has work in development with Hat Trick Productions. She was recently the RSC Writer on Attachment and part of the Channel 4Screenwriters' Course.

EMMA CALLANDER | Director
Emma is the Artistic Director of Theatre Uncut. She trained at the National Theatre of Scotland on the Regional Theatre Young Directors Scheme. Work for Theatre Uncut includes *The Merthyr Stigmatist* by Lisa Parry and *Bubble* by Kieran Hurley. She has directed Theatre Uncut shorts at the Young Vic, Traverse Theatre, Bristol Old Vic Theatre, Arches Glasgow and Teatr Grob Copenhagen. Work as Associate Director for the Traverse Theatre includes *Cuckooed* by Mark Thomas and *Crash* by Andy Duffy. She has won three Fringe Firsts, the Herald Angel, Spirit of the Fringe and the Amnesty International Freedom of Expression Award.

HAZEL LOW | Designer
Hazel Low is a performance designer and collaborator across theatre, live art and spatial design. Recent Credits: *The Legend of Ned Ludd*, Liverpool Everyman. *Succession Theme is my Ringtone*, Rose Theatre; *Tiger*, Omnibus Theatre; *Bonfire*, Derby Theatre, Sheffield Theatre, Non Such. *As We Face The Sun* and *Pass It On*, Bush Theatre; *Who Killed My Father*, Tron Theatre, Summerhall, and Scottish Tour (co-design with Blythe Brett). *The Suicide*, Sainsbury Theatre LAMDA; *Splintered*, Soho Theatre; *Brilliant Jerks*, Southwark Playhouse; *Paradise Now*, Bush Theatre (as co-costume designer and design associate); *I, Joan*, Shakespeare's Globe (as design associate); *Bogeyman*, Pleasance Queendome; *The Blue House*, Blue Elephant Theatre; *The Magic Flute*, Royal College of Music (co-designed with Rosie Elnile); *Trainers*, Gate Theatre (as design assistant). Spatial design projects include NDT Broadgate (as Design Associate) and the Royal Court's pop up bar Court in the Square in 2020.

ROLY BOTHA | Composer & Sound Designer
Roly (they/them) is a composer and sound designer, and is an Associate Artist of The PappyShow. Theatre includes: *Gunter* (Royal Court); *Dear Young Monster* (Bristol Old Vic); *Hir* (Park); *Gwyneth Goes Skiing* (Pleasance); *Truth & Tails* (Chichester Festival Theatre); *Tambo & Bones* (Theatre Royal Stratford East); *Shut Up, I'm Dreaming* (National Theatre/School's Tour); *The Ultimate Pickle*, *A Sudden Violent Burst of Rain*, *Half-Empty Glasses* (Paines Plough); *Orlando* (Jermyn Street); *BOYS* (Barbican, Southbank Centre, touring); *Coming To England* (Birmingham Rep); *WILD* (Unicorn); *Blowhole* (Soho); *Milk & Gall* (Theatre503); *Brother* (Southwark Playhouse); and *Warheads* (Park – Olivier Nominated).

KATE BONNEY | Lighting Designer
Kate designs lighting for a wide variety of live performance and events. Her heart lies in creating work that audiences never forget alongside telling stories that deserve to be told. Recent credits include *So Young* with the Traverse Theatre, *Old Boy* with Dundee Rep, *Cyprus Avenue* with the Tron and *Mimi Store* with Jupiter+ on Perth High Street. Kate

also forms half of design company Lightworks Events Ltd alongside Simon Hayes. Together they led the design of *Enchanted Forest* from 2013 until 2019, designed *My Light Shines On* with Edinburgh International Festival in 2020 during the peak of the pandemic and last year found themselves designing lighting a vertical launch space vehicle (a rocket) for a large scale photoshoot with Orbex, an aerospace company based in Kate's hometown of Forres, Moray.

ALINE DAVID | Movement Director & Choreographer

Theatre work includes: *Till the Stars Come Down*; *A Taste of Honey*; *Barber Shop Chronicles*; *Romeo and Juliet*; *Emil and the Detectives*; *Antigone*; *The Kitchen*; *Greenland and Our Class* (all National Theatre); *Arabian Nights* (Bristol Old Vic) *The Cord*; *The Arrival* (The Bush Theatre); *Sons of the Prophet* (Hampstead Theatre); *The Brothers Size*; *Dutchman*; *Eurydice*; *Elektra*; *Parallel Macbeth*; *The Invisible Woman; Playsize* (all Young Vic); *Wedding Band*; *School Girls Or, The African Mean Girls Play* (Lyric Hammersmith); *Dance Nation; The House of Bernarda Alba* (both Almeida); *Macbeth; The Merchant of Venice* (both RSC); *Gunter; Gone Too Far!*; *Wanderlust* (all Royal Court); *The Iphigenia Quartet*; *How to be Another Woman* (both Gate); *First Love is the Revolution*; *FLIP!* (Soho Theatre); *The Crucible*; *Romeo and Juliet*; *A Taste of Honey*; *Alice* (all Sheffield Crucible); *Of Mice and Men* (Birmingham Rep); *Looking for Yogurt* (Birmingham Studio); *Henry VIII*; *Romeo and Juliet*; *Women Beware Women*; *Antony & Cleopatra*; *Much Ado About Nothing*; *Troilus and Cressida; Handel and the First Messiah* (all Shakespeare's Globe); *Proof* (Menier Chocolate Factory); *Waiting for Godot* (West Yorkshire Playhouse); *1984*; *Macbeth; The Mighty Waltzer* (all Royal Exchange); *A Christmas Carol* (Sherman; Cardiff); *The Owl and the Pussycat* (ROH Olympic Project); *Working* (Royal Academy of Music); *Nothing* (Glyndebourne/Den Jyske Opera) and *Daphne* (La Monnaie; Belgium). Television work includes: *The Crown S5*; *The Crown S6* (Netflix); *Augustus* (Apple); *The Typist* (Sky Arts).

ADAM JEFFERYS | Production Manager

Adam Jefferys is a Lighting Designer and Production Manager from Essex.
Recent work: *My Fathers Fable* (Bush); *The Bleeding Tree, Under The Kundè Tree* (both Southwark); *The Great Privation* (Theatre503); *The Olive Boy* (UK Tour); *Murder In The Dark* (UK Tour); *Elephant* (Bush); *It Is I, Seagull* (UK Tour); *Soon, Pilot* (both Summerhall); *Philosophy of The World* (Cambridge Junction); *After The Act, War & Culture* (both New Diorama); *Project Dictator* (New Diorama & Edinburgh); *Jekyll and Hyde* (Derby); *Everything Has Changed* (Tour & Edinburgh); *Dorian* (Reading Rep).
For more of Adam's work please visit his website: adamjefferys.com

IONA HICKS | Stage Manager

A recent graduate of Bristol Old Vic Theatre School, Iona specialised in Stage Management during her final year. She recently completed a five week placement at the Donmar Warehouse as the Stage Management Intern on *Macbeth*, directed by Max Webster. Iona has also worked as SM on tour for Sam Wilde's *Boxville*.

Credits while in training include:

As Stage Manager: *A Very Expensive Poison* (Circomedia); *The Nobodies* (The Wardrobe); *Scenes with Girls* (The Wardrobe).

Deputy Stage Manager: *Jekyll & Hyde* (Tobacco Factory Theatres).

Assistant Stage Manager: *This House* (Tobacco Factory Theatres); *Henry IV* (Bristol Old Vic, Weston Studio).

Construction Assistant: *Catastrophe Bay* (Bristol Old Vic, Main Stage); *Loam* (Bristol Old Vic, Main Stage).

Grace Dickson Productions (GDP) is a bold new production company, developing and producing formally innovative & bitingly relevant new writing that champions marginalised voices. GDP works collaboratively with artists on professional development as well as producing work that isn't afraid to make a noise and ruffle some feathers. GDP produces theatre that represents the world we live in and the worlds beyond it; work that is imaginative, playful and boundary-breaking.

Previous collaborations include: *Rhum + Clay*, *The REcreate Agency* (Park Theatre); *Bric A Brac* (Freight Theatre, Ransack Theatre & Silent Faces), at venues such as Park Theatre, New Diorama, Soho Theatre, Southwark Playhouse, Roundhouse and on tour.

GDP encompasses the work of Grace Dickson, a Newcastle-born producer with a keen eye for powerful, socially relevant new writing. Grace works across the industry in roles including Associate Producer at Francesca Moody Productions (for whom she line produced *Feeling Afraid As If Something Terrible Is Going To Happen* at the Bush Theatre and Tim Crouch's *An Oak Tree* internationally) Accounts Assistant/ Bookkeeper at Runaway Entertainment & co-founder of HD General Management with Ameena Hamid. Her recent work is supported by the Stage One Bursary for New Producers.

Credits include: *Lady Dealer* (Roundabout, Bush Theatre); *The Long Run* (New Diorama); *Splintered* (Soho Theatre); *Project Dictator* (New Diorama); *Move Fast and Break Things* (Summerhall, Edinburgh Fringe; *Bogeyman* (Pleasance Edinburgh Fringe) and *Belly Up* (Turbine Theatre).

www.gracedicksonproductions.co.uk

THEATRE
UNCUT

Theatre Uncut creates bold, progressive, uncompromising political theatre for live and digital audiences across the world.

We galvanise action and fuel debate by supporting the world's leading playwrights and extraordinary new voices to create political writing that raises awareness on issues of social injustice.

We then make this work available for anyone to perform anywhere. Over 200,000 people across 26 countries have performed Theatre Uncut plays so far.

We believe that theatre has the power to make positive social change.

www.theatreuncut.com

CHARACTERS

KEIRA – She's explosive and electric in her vulgarity. Her capacity for extreme emotion means she has an animalistic approach to love and loyalty. She would take on a thousand armies for her mates. Loudest in any room, she's like a stand up set on a stage that could collapse any second.

ZAINAB – Pragmatic, methodical and mature. She's not a prude, she's Earth.

LUCY – She's like a cloud with legs. Receptive, eager to learn and vulnerable in her curiosity. Perhaps Lucy fell out of a rabbit hole, or she's just a product of someone poked about by a Church. Either way, she has a brightness. She's Air.

SETTING

The play is set in an unidentified town in the West Midlands. Having said that, this could happen in any town, anywhere. It isn't necessary for the actors to share a particular dialect or accent. All the action happens at the base of an oak tree.

AUTHOR'S NOTES

Punctuation isn't always grammatical.
New thoughts sometimes appear on new lines.
/ indicates overlapping dialogue.

A gentle steer to actors: the play lives and dies on pace. Go quick! These girls are certain, curious and rarely sentimental.

THANKS

The production would like to thank Shoreditch Town Hall, Tanya Folllett and the team at Bristol Old Vic, Bush Theatre, Joanna Kennedy, Rutger Bellaerts, Letty Thomas, Harry Elletson, SM Publicity and Thread Design.

The production is proudly supported by public funding from Arts Council England and by the Stage One Bursary for New Producers

FOREWORD

This was my first play and it was an absolute bollock to write. Before acknowledging everyone who made it possible, I thought I'd write a bit about where it came from. The development of *Playfight* took years, but the first ten pages took ten minutes and have remained untouched(ish) since the beginning.

The 'sex game gone wrong defence' was brought to my attention in 2019 at a birthday picnic. My friend's mum had read an article written in response to the death of Grace Millane. Grace had been backpacking around New Zealand and had been strangled to death by her Tinder date on the eve of her birthday. Her date had then sat in their hotel room, photographed her dead body and watched porn. He later put her body in a suitcase and buried it in the woods and was now in court claiming she was into rough sex and had therefore consented.

We sang happy birthday to my friend and I went to my bar shift at the Royal Court. I'd been really rocked by what I'd heard. It brought up lots of thoughts and feelings I guess we're conditioned to suppress as kids in order to be perceived as light-hearted and desirable. When I got home that night I wrote the first ten pages of *Playfight*. Later that year, when offered a place on the Royal Court's introduction to playwriting group, I knew what I wanted to write about.

The play doesn't seek to land on any answers. Or to shame or blame anyone who safely practices breath play and kinks. The play seeks to wrestle with the deep trauma of expectation. How we're tossed about in an education system that favours prime numbers over how to look after ourselves in a terrifying world. How we force our bodies into uncomfortable shapes like they do on the screens. How dangerously we drift from ourselves. I guess it's a cry for change. What that change looks like I haven't got a clue. But this is my attempt at kicking the door open to the conversation.

After all that, I really hope you find moments of joy in the play.

ACKNOWLEDGEMENTS

Playfight marks the start of a turbulent relationship with a bastard profession and I really could not have done it without the following people, who gave their thoughts and feedback. And to those that keep me swimming on the surface and happy.

Susan Edwards, Susan is a barrister who sat with me opposite the Central Criminal Court with her heels in her handbag, and went through the current legislation surrounding the sex game gone wrong defence. It was September 2019 and she was pushing for the legislation in England to change. At the time I thought I would be writing a sort of courtroom drama. But my chat with Susan right at the start of the process convinced me that the social context beyond the courtroom should be the central focus of the play. We talked about our upbringings, about sex, porn and friendships. Thanks to her and others, the fifty shades sex game defence was abolished in England in 2020, while I was on my 50,000th draft. Not so in Scotland though.

Oli Lansley, Oli, thank you so much. Oli is an amazing theatre maker/ writer and he read a very early draft of *Playfight* when it was just themes and ideas. He reminded me of the importance of story. Why are we meeting these characters now? What's happened? What is going to happen? It's something I come back to all the time. What is the actual story? The other thing Oli taught me (and it is the BEST advice for any writer) is: if you're feeling stuck, walk away and FILL UP YOUR CUP. See friends, go to the pub, read about the subject you're exploring, listen to music that sounds like the inside of the characters, go to an exhibition, see a film. Dance round the edges of the play's world until your cup is full. Then kick it over and go again.

Royal Court Theatre (Myah Jeffers, Ellie Fulcher, Jane Fallowfield) Thank you for giving me a place on your course. It gave me the confidence and space to make something. Thank you for reading harrowing early drafts. Thank you for teaching me that words can't always say the thing. Sometimes a painting of a lamb giving birth to a planet gives the energy of a mad moment in the play. Till the words come. If they do.

Wildcard Theatre Company: Em Stott and the Jets. Thank you for hosting a readthrough of *Playfight*. Beth Kapila, thank you for directing it. To George and Chris at Papatango, shortlisting me for that award was enough validation for a lifetime. Thank you. Neil McPherson and the Finborough Theatre. Winning the ETPEP Award gave me a huge kick start in the industry and I'm forever grateful for your support and encouragement. Blanche McIntyre, thank you for sitting on Zoom with me for five billion hours helping bring that reading to life. To Charlie Coulthard at Concord Theatricals, for all the checking in and support and for suggesting me to a writing agent. Enter: Alec Drysdale, who took me on after reading *Playfight* all those years ago. You are my biggest support system, I love you and Bryn Chiappe very much. To Concord Theatricals, thank you for publishing this. Full circle moment, eh? To all the actors who over the years read various drafts out loud, your insights and energy have kicked up sparks that helped to shape the play: Hannah Millward, Fanta Barrie, Nadi Kemp-Sayfi, Helen Monks, Robyn Cara, Libby Mai.

Nina Cassells, Sophie Cox and Lucy Mangan - here we go! Thank you for breathing life into these girls. I can't wait to see what you do with them. Thank you for your bravery and beauty.

The biggest thank you to Emma Callander and Grace Dickson. You two stuck with the play for four years. When we didn't get funding, you had to make tough decisions but always protected my heart and kept faith. Thank you for your generosity, passion, commitment and belly laughs. You are very magical people. Emma, thank you for ringing me from the weirdest nooks of the UK and putting so much passion into the story. You have been the most important shaper and maker of this. I really cannot thank you enough. Grace, thank you for your consistency, curiosity and grounded energy. You are a phenomenal producer, and a dear friend. Thank you for everything over the years.

To Rachel Lemon and Lydia Higman. The Dirty Hare bunnies. Making theatre with you both has changed my life. I love you both so much. You are endlessly supportive and I am always fascinated by what comes out of your brains and hearts. Thank you for all the half pints, petrol tanks and peeling walls in weird rehearsal spaces. And for reading *Playfight* and giving me your thoughts and feelings. Here's to many more years of making!

To my friends I grew up with and who have supported me while making this. Liv, I know living with a mopey out-of-work playwright must have been so fucking annoying. Thank you for filling the flat with laughs and roast chicken. I chose to set *Playfight* around the base of a tree like the one outside our school. Lyd for coming to read throughs and forcing loud laughter. You're my rock. Oscar who gave me lots of hugs when we weren't able to get the play up last year. Anna and Jess, thank you for walking through life with me in your purple uniforms when we all got heckled as 'purple virgins' on our way to school.

Wendy Higman for bringing this subject matter to my attention at the birthday picnic in 2019 and for all your wise words and baking over the years.

To Cheryl Prince and Lauren Dickson. I'm so proud of you both. We were polishing cutlery behind the bar when this was just an idea. You always listened and inspired me. You still do now.

Mum, you're the most supportive bundle of love in the world. Dad, you're the best dad ever and I'm so happy to include your amazing poem about a tree in this play text and to my sister, Philly, you're the most chaotic meteorite of wonder ever to hit the planet.

And lastly, this play is, of course, unwaveringly dedicated to Grace Millane.

This ancient oak,
Over the centuries,
What hasn't it heard – from those under its branches – what hasn't
it felt or seen?
Love it has seen a million times no doubt,
Heard hatred too,
And in its heart of oak felt too perhaps a millions times
our echoed doubts
and echoed fears
and all our echoed inner pain.

Simon Grogan

(An oak tree. It's centuries old. Seen it all. Even if we can only touch its trunk, we are aware of the oak's roots stretching deep into the soil – as deep as its branches stretch high – into infinity.)

*(**ZAINAB** appears from behind it.)*

ZAINAB. I've been thinking about time.

Every second.

I think about time.

I think about the time it took.

I think about the time that's passed.

I can't stop thinking about the time in-between.

The ugly bits. The fuzzy bits. The bits so shameful you feel your knickers shimmy down your legs and bury themselves underground.

The spaces. Gaps in time –

I can't stop thinking about them.

(She leans against the tree.)

So I'll be here.

When the world's spinning round. Swear down, I'll be here.

(She looks up at the branches above.)

Where time stands still. Just for a second. And that second.

It's bliss. Isn't it?

*

(The base of our tree, spring 2015.)

*(Three fifteen-year-old girls in school uniform. **KEIRA**, **ZAINAB,** and **LUCY**. They are staring at a dead squirrel. It's been strangled in the plastic rings of a six-pack of beer.)*

LUCY. Nasty way to go.

ZAINAB. Wonder how long it's been here.

LUCY. Reckon it's got a family?

ZAINAB. Probably.

LUCY. Reckon they'll be waiting for it?

ZAINAB. Probably.

KEIRA. It's a squirrel not a fucking choir boy.

LUCY. So?

KEIRA. So happens all the time.

LUCY. Wonder if its soul is flying above us seeking vengeance on the killer.

KEIRA. Are you taking the piss?

LUCY. What?

KEIRA. It's been choked by a plastic beer pack.

LUCY. So.

KEIRA. It probably fancied a bevvy.

ZAINAB. Even if it did. Didn't ask for this, did it.

LUCY. No something's gone on here.

KEIRA. Probably killed itself 'cause this school's so peak.

LUCY. *(Gasps clutches her throat.)* It couldn't breathe.

(Beat.)

KEIRA. Do you want a tissue mate?

LUCY. Oo, it's got a tiny knob –

KEIRA. Right, stop having a clit rub over a squirrel. Do you want to hear the end of my story or not?

ZAINAB. Go on then.

KEIRA. So the bouncer was like, alright just this once, but if you're not back in ten minutes, you're not allowed back in. So don't take the piss.

LUCY. How come he let you do that?

KEIRA. Told him I needed ciggies and flashed him a nipple.

ZAINAB. You're lying.

KEIRA. Am not. Ask Dan Miller.

ZAINAB. How did you get in in the first place?

KEIRA. ID. Found Miss Preston's in the car park.

ZAINAB. Are you taking the piss? She's forty-five.

KEIRA. So? Wore a push up bra.

ZAINAB. And she's Sri Lankan. So bollocks you got away with that.

KEIRA. Honest. Just handed it over, told him I had a hairless vagina and passed the 11+.

ZAINAB. Bollocks did that work.

KEIRA. It did. Got a stamp to prove it, look.

*(**KEIRA** presents her wrist, **LUCY** admires it.)*

LUCY. Ooh yeah. Look at that. What does it say?

KEIRA. Cock magnet. It's a bit smudged.

LUCY. Thought the club was called *Smack*?

KEIRA. Yeah it is.

LUCY. So why does it say that?

KEIRA. Dunno. Sounds cool.

LUCY. *(Thinking...)* Cock magnet. *(Nods.)* Yeah suppose.

KEIRA. Had four vodka red bulls for two quid. Drank so many thought I was gonna have a heart attack. Just like explode. Then right, he came over, rubbed his knob against my leg –

LUCY. Who?

KEIRA. Barack Obama, who'd you think?

LUCY. Oh yeah.

KEIRA. And said, do you wanna bone? And I was like, yeah.

ZAINAB. Woah. Bit forward.

KEIRA. Yeah but Dan's eighteen so it's different isn't it. He's mature. Got proper experience and that.

ZAINAB. Isn't that a bit...

KEIRA. Bit what?

ZAINAB. Bit weird?

KEIRA. Why?

ZAINAB. 'Cause you're fifteen.

KEIRA. Yeah but he doesn't know that, does he.

ZAINAB. Still. Doesn't that make him, like, a kiddy fiddler?

LUCY. Oh that's a thought.

KEIRA. What's a thought?

LUCY. That Dan Miller is a kiddy fiddler.

(Beat.)

KEIRA. Right so we were at the club…

ZAINAB. Yeah…

KEIRA. We left the club…

LUCY. Yeah…

KEIRA. And we had sex on the tennis courts.

ZAINAB. What?

LUCY. You never.

KEIRA. We did. Doggy style.

LUCY. *(Wonderment.)* Doggy style?

KEIRA. Yeah. Do you wanna see?

ZAINAB. What?

KEIRA. I filmed it. Looked great. Apart from the awkward bit.

ZAINAB. The awkward bit?

KEIRA. Well. He asked to smack me in the face.

ZAINAB. That is awkward.

KEIRA. That's not the awkward bit. Was awkward 'cause I had to say no.

LUCY. Why did you have to say no?

KEIRA. Everyone knows I live in a bungalow and you can't say you've fallen down the stairs if you've got none?

LUCY. Fairs.

ZAINAB. Why did he want to hit you? Had you upset him?

KEIRA. Nah. Just a thing isn't it. Both just started laughing. My knees were really cut up. Sandy tennis floor. Savage. Bled all the way back to the club. Was a bit weird. 'Cause Dan went from full on laughing to like full on crying. Proper howling like a wounded animal. So pretended I didn't know him and just started dancing again. Then right, was in the smoking area, and that twat Lisa Wallis came over and was like mate you've got blood running down your legs. What happened? And I was like fuck it, so I told her. She was like whaaaat? Bollocks! So I sent her the video to prove it.

(**LUCY** *leans forward.*)

LUCY. What did she say?

KEIRA. She said. Welcome to the club. Bought me a tequila and everything.

LUCY. Lisa Wallis bought you a tequila? That's sick.

KEIRA. I'm a proper woman now. Felt all holy and shit.

ZAINAB. Being doggied on a tennis court felt holy?

KEIRA. Yeah symbolic. Now I know why you're in church so much Lucy. To see Jesus and his two incher.

LUCY. What did it feel like?

KEIRA. Climactic. Felt like I was a fantasy. Didn't feel real.

LUCY. Woah.

(*Beat.*)

Scares me.

KEIRA. What?

LUCY. Penis.

KEIRA. Lesbian.

LUCY. Am not.

KEIRA. It's not that scary. You'd be surprised how much you just know. Animal instincts. Well that and like the videos and stuff. Stick to the classics; Cream Pie Carley, Sasha Grey, Fake Taxi. You just sort of copy them. Like a dance mat.

LUCY. I'm good on a dance mat.

KEIRA. Yeah you are to be fair, so you'll be fine. Zainab you're shit on one so you'll be shit in bed.

ZAINAB. I'm dyspraxic.

KEIRA. So?

ZAINAB. So don't take the piss?

KEIRA. You two should have come out.

LUCY. We were watching *Blue Planet* with Zainab's mum.

    (Beat.)

KEIRA. Wait what?

LUCY. What?

KEIRA. Cheers for the invite.

ZAINAB. Didn't think you'd want to come.

KEIRA. Would have been nice to be asked.

LUCY. Oh. Sorry.

ZAINAB. You know what my mum's like.

KEIRA. Whatever. Might go and bosh one out in the toilets.

ZAINAB. Nice.

    (The three girls look down at the squirrel.)

KEIRA. Shall we lob this off into the field then?

    (Beat.)

ALL. Shotgun not.

*

LUCY. Been trying all night. Hardly slept.

ZAINAB. Oh. Right. Well. Wouldn't wind yourself up about it.

LUCY. But I'll never feel it.

ZAINAB. Feel what?

LUCY. The climactic stuff.

ZAINAB. Well. What are you...like doing?

LUCY. Two fingers either side and rubbing it round and round and round and round and round in circles.

ZAINAB. Then what?

LUCY. Then get the fuzzy feeling. Feels like I've drank a coffee or I'm being chased by a goose, like scared but also quite excited, start getting all breathless and that and it's building and building and building and building – and then I think of Jesus and it just stops.

> *(Beat.)*

ZAINAB. Well maybe try and think of someone else –

LUCY. Even tried rubbing it on the clamp in DT.

ZAINAB. And?

LUCY. Nothing.

> *(Beat.)*

ZAINAB. I'm sure you're just overthinking it. Getting trapped in your head.

LUCY. Said a prayer this morning. So that might sort things out.

> *(**ZAINAB** starts tight roping on a tree root.)*

ZAINAB. Got a spare one?

LUCY. What?

ZAINAB. Prayer.

LUCY. What do you need?

ZAINAB. Decent GCSEs. Get mum off my back.

(**LUCY** *side eyes her.*)

LUCY. What do you actually need?

(*Beat.*)

ZAINAB. Remember when you used to lick my shoulder in primary school?

LUCY. Uh. A bit.

(**ZAINAB** *wobbles,* **LUCY** *holds her hand to steady her.*)

ZAINAB. Weird isn't it. That you believe in something I don't.

LUCY. Suppose. It's all we had when my dad died.

(**LUCY** *shrugs.*)

I like it. Being commanded. You should try it.

ZAINAB. Nah...

(*Beat.*)

LUCY. You could talk to tree!

ZAINAB. Eh?

LUCY. Tree. It's just the same. Tree listens.

(*She pats the trunk. Whispers –*)

Sometimes think it knows all the answers.

(**ZAINAB** *studies the back of* **LUCY** *like she's a crazy imp.*)

ZAINAB. Cheers. I'll bear that in mind –

LUCY. You spoken to Keira?

ZAINAB. Not today. Why?

LUCY. She's been asked to see the Head. Think it's with Lisa too.

ZAINAB. Oh right.

LUCY. Have you watched it?

ZAINAB. No. That's weird.

LUCY. Yeah. Suppose.

Reckon Dan will get told off?

ZAINAB. Doubt that. Can't really pick on one person when everyone's at it, can you.

LUCY. Reckon they were too harsh on Ted Bundy then?

ZAINAB. Nah Luce. He deserved that one.

(*Beat.*)

LUCY. Do *you* ever get the fuzzy feeling?

ZAINAB. ... Yeah.

LUCY. You cum before?

ZAINAB. Yeah.

LUCY. What does it feel like?

(**ZAINAB** *looks at* **LUCY**, *shifts uncomfortably.*)

ZAINAB. Feels good. Feel all the tension squeezing my bones together just melt away. And when it stops, I get these weird shivers. Like a ghost is passing through me.

(*Beat.*)

(**LUCY** *gasps in awe.*)

*

(**KEIRA** *is looking up at the branches.* **ZAINAB** *enters. Watches her for a second. Then –*)

ZAINAB. What you doing?

KEIRA. Waiting.

ZAINAB. For what?

KEIRA. The bus.

ZAINAB. What happened to the last bus?

KEIRA. I got off it.

    (Beat.)

ZAINAB. Just put your headphones in. Ignore them. It's just a video.

    (Beat.)

KEIRA. Reckon I could stay over?

ZAINAB. It's a school night. Exams.

KEIRA. So?

ZAINAB. So, can't you just go home?

KEIRA. Dad's got AA. Can't be arsed to wait in the car. Like a labrador.

ZAINAB. What are you in the car for?

KEIRA. Get bored on my own.

ZAINAB. Come on. You're nearly sixteen.

KEIRA. So?

ZAINAB. So not a kiddy anymore.

KEIRA. Alright cheers, Nanny McPhee.

ZAINAB. Just saying.

    (Beat.)

KEIRA. Well. Whatever. Like the smell of cars anyway. Hot leather.

(Beat.)

ZAINAB. Mum's here. You sure you're alright for the bus?

KEIRA. I'll be sound.

> *(**ZAINAB** goes. **KEIRA** looks back up to the tree, studying it.)*

> *

> *(The three are sitting under the tree. **LUCY** is leaning on its base, **ZAINAB** propped up next to her. They're watching **KEIRA**, who is facing away from them. Looking at her phone screen with headphones.)*

> *(Silence. Then.)*

LUCY. Has she changed pill?

ZAINAB. Yeah. Microgynon didn't grow her tits apparently.

Do you wanna go to the fields tonight? Mercury's passing through Venus and Jupiter. They're calling it dance of the planets. Meant to look mental.

LUCY. Yeah alright then.

> *(**ZAINAB** smiles –)*

You gonna come Keira?

> *(Deflates.)*

ZAINAB. She can't hear you.

> *(**LUCY** crawls over, thumps her in the leg. Peers at her screen.)*

LUCY. Eugh. What you watching that for? It's the middle of the day.

> *(**KEIRA** rears round, pulls out her headphones.)*

KEIRA. Why you snooping?

ZAINAB. What is it?

KEIRA. None of your business.

LUCY. Is that porn –

KEIRA. Yes. Lucy. Yes it is.

ZAINAB. What you watching that for?

KEIRA. Because I feel like it. Because hanging out with you two, I can honestly feel my sperm count dropping.

ZAINAB. Eh?

KEIRA. Just –

> (**KEIRA** *stands. Tries to make sense of something with her hands. Erratic.)*

ZAINAB. You alright?

KEIRA. No! No I'm not 'alright'. Look at us. We look like three virgins on a hill. All we need is a fucking custard making hoover. No one's going to want to bang me again if you guys behave like you are right now. We need to step our pussies up. Think of priorities. Can't wear thick tights forever.

LUCY. Have to. Got bad circulation.

KEIRA. It won't work in your favour Luce. You need to look like you've seen things. Like you pay taxes and can fit a cock up your bum.

ZAINAB. Ah what?

KEIRA. She won't get a boyfriend looking like a Jehovah's Witness. At least not a decent one, and you deserve more than decent Lucy. You're magic. You're so fucking magic. You deserve the best.

LUCY. Chapter fourteen. And that which fell among thorns are they, which, when they have heard, go forth, and are choked with cares and riches and pleasures of this life, and bring no fruit to perfection.

Luke.

KEIRA. He at boys school?

ZAINAB. He's one of Jesus's disciples.

LUCY. Means stop being so desperate to have sex with everything.

KEIRA. Can you hear yourself? You sound like a crusty old nan. We're going sixth form next year. Need to have fucked at least twenty blokes. Come on. Can't be Saint Lucy forever.

LUCY. Who?

KEIRA. Saint Lucy. The Virgin Lucy. Lucy who can't get no juicy.

LUCY. I can get juicy. Been fingered behind church before.

ZAINAB. What? When?

(**ZAINAB** *looks at* **LUCY**, *a bit crushed.*)

LUCY. Couple of months back. Mothering Sunday.

ZAINAB. Who was it?

LUCY. Eric.

ZAINAB. Who's Eric?

LUCY. He's a tenor. Well his balls dropped, so he's now a baritone. Felt alright. But none of this out-of-body-experience stuff you go on about. Had to pull out my tampon sneakily and fling it off into the gravestones. Don't think he noticed.

ZAINAB. Was it romantic?

KEIRA. Fuck sake.

LUCY. A bit. Pretended to cum and then we ate biscuits in the chapel.

>   (*Beat.*)

Reckon we'll get married one day.

>   (*A light goes out in* **ZAINAB**.)

KEIRA. Oh here we go…

LUCY. Don't take the piss –

KEIRA. Christians getting horny, bored and married at fifteen.

LUCY. Not that –

KEIRA. Tale as old as time.

LUCY. You just don't understand it.

KEIRA. Yeah because I'm not medieval.

>   (*Stiff beat,* **ZAINAB** *studies* **KEIRA**.)

ZAINAB. How was your meeting?

KEIRA. Eh?

ZAINAB. What was it about?

>   (**KEIRA** *goes back to put her headphones in.*
>   **LUCY** *looks at* **ZAINAB**. *Then –*)

LUCY. Was it about Dan?

>   (**KEIRA** *stops moving.*)

KEIRA. How did you hear about Dan?

LUCY. Just a guess. Think he's having a rough one. After… you know. Feel a bit bad for him really.

>   (*Beat.*)

Been thinking maybe you should say sorry?

Like. I dunno. Maybe it wasn't a good idea saying you were eighteen. And like sharing the video and stuff.

(*Beat.*)

KEIRA. Are you taking the piss?

ZAINAB. Could just say sorry. Get people off his back.

(**KEIRA** *starts packing up her things.*)

LUCY. Didn't mean to upset you. Was just saying –

KEIRA. Well fucking don't –

LUCY. Just saying incase, you know –

KEIRA. I said leave it Lucy –

LUCY. Just might make everything a bit easier –

KEIRA. It's a bit fucking late for that.

ZAINAB. Why?

KEIRA. Because Dan's killed himself.

(*Beat.*)

Because he's fucking dead.

*

(**LUCY** *and* **ZAINAB** *enter.*)

LUCY. ... Well I thought it was quite perky.

ZAINAB. Course *you* did. Seeing every school kid in town flocking outside your church.

LUCY. It was beautiful.

ZAINAB. Everyone singing Amazing Grace.

LUCY. And that projector screen. Didn't know we had one of those. Imagine being so popular your funeral gets its own live outdoor screening. For the masses.

ZAINAB. Was like a drive in cinema.

LUCY. Can you make sure I get one of those. If I die. When I die.

ZAINAB. I'll try my best.

LUCY. And when his sister sang that solo –

ZAINAB. I thought you were going to have a multiple orgasm.

LUCY. Raw nerve.

ZAINAB. Sorry. *(Tannoy voice.)* Splash zone in pew five.

LUCY. It's my favourite song.

ZAINAB. Which one?

LUCY. Make Me a Channel of Your Peace. You know.

> *(Sung rapidly.)*

MAKE ME A CHANNEL OF YOUR PEACE
WHERE THERE IS HATRED, LET ME BRING YOUR LOVE
WHERE THERE IS INJURY, YOUR PARDON LORD
ANDWHERETHERE'SDOUBT, TRUEFAITHINYOU –

> *(Pause. **ZAINAB** smiles at her.)*

What?

ZAINAB. Keep going.

> *(**LUCY** reluctantly sings, suddenly aware of herself. **ZAINAB** just watches her.)*

LUCY. *(Sung.)*

OH MASTER, GRANT THAT I MAY NEVER SEEK
SO MUCH TO BE CONSOLED AS TO CONSOLE
TO BE UNDERSTOOD AS TO UNDERSTAND
TO BE LOVED AS TO LOVE WITH ALL MY SOUL.

> *(Beat.)*

ZAINAB. Shame Keira didn't show. Somehow didn't feel right without her.

LUCY. Yeah. I think that would have been tough.

Kept thinking I was going to laugh. Not because I wasn't sad. But like. When things are that horrific. It's almost funny isn't it. Like you'd have to laugh or you'd just kill yourself.

> (**ZAINAB** *side eyes her.*)

ZAINAB. Felt guilty for being there.

LUCY. Why?

ZAINAB. Churches just make me feel guilty.

LUCY. Sort of get what you mean.

ZAINAB. Really?

LUCY. Yeah. The Holy Trinity.

Shame, blame and guilt.

> (*Pause.*)

ZAINAB. I had a mental one last night.

LUCY. Oh yeah?

ZAINAB. Swear you won't laugh?

LUCY. Swear.

> (*Beat.*)

ZAINAB. Was watching a programme about Henry VIII with mum. About all his wives and how they used to need a crane to lift him out the bath and that.

> (**LUCY**'s *eyes widen...*)

And there was this scene where like Anne Boleyn was about to be beheaded. She was leaning down, against the block. And you could see right down her dress –

LUCY. Woah.

ZAINAB. What?

LUCY. That *is* mental.

ZAINAB. What? I haven't said it yet –

LUCY. Oh. Right.

>   (**ZAINAB** *swallows, recomposing nervously.*)

ZAINAB. And I felt something in –

LUCY. They had to use a crane did they?

ZAINAB. Luce –

LUCY. Sorry.

>   (*Beat.*)

ZAINAB. You could see right down. Was all sweaty. And. Well, they were boobs. Obviously. And I felt something in me. Like wob. Felt my knickers get a bit. You know. Told mum I needed a piss, ran upstairs and...

>   (*Beat.*)

And I lay there afterwards. Could feel my heartbeat in my ears.

Felt. Great.

>   (*Beat.*)

>   (**LUCY** *smuggles a laugh.*)

It's not funny.

LUCY. Sorry. No. Just –

ZAINAB. What?

LUCY. You having a wank to Anne Boleyn. Getting her head cut off.

ZAINAB. Yeah, alright.

LUCY. I reckon you're eating chocolate before bed. You get proper mental thoughts if you do that.

ZAINAB. Don't think it's that.

LUCY. Well what is it then?

> *(Beat.)*

ZAINAB. I think I like.

LUCY. Who?

ZAINAB. Girls.

> *(Pause.)*

LUCY. You gonna tell your mum?

ZAINAB. Have you met my mum? She'd go skits. Should've seen her in Morrisons car park.

LUCY. Morrisons car park?

ZAINAB. Yeah. Morrisons car park.

LUCY. What happened in Morrisons car park?

ZAINAB. Well. We were in Morrisons car park –

LUCY. Yeah got that bit.

ZAINAB. And these two girls walked out. Holding hands. She wound down the window. Called them a fucking disgrace.

LUCY. Oh. Right.

> (**LUCY** *lies her head on* **ZAINAB**'s *lap, looking up at the leaves.* **ZAINAB** *looks down at her.*)

ZAINAB. You alright?

LUCY. Yeah.

> *(Beat.)*

Think I might write a poem.

ZAINAB. About what?

LUCY. About Tree.

*

*(Three a.m. The bubble tone of a video call going through. **KEIRA** is sitting underneath the tree. The light from her phone sharp against her face. **ZAINAB**'s voice is tinny through the phone.)*

ZAINAB. You alright mate?

KEIRA. Yeah. Just fancied a catch up.

ZAINAB. It's three in the morning.

KEIRA. Ah what? Is it?

ZAINAB. Are you at school?

KEIRA. Are you a lesbian?

ZAINAB. I think so. Yeah.

KEIRA. Cool.

(Beat.)

How did that come about?

ZAINAB. What do you mean?

KEIRA. When did you turn into one of them?

ZAINAB. Doesn't really work like that. Think I came out the womb one.

KEIRA. Oh right. Yeah. Course.

ZAINAB. You okay about it?

(Beat.)

KEIRA. Why wouldn't I be? If anyone gives you shit for it. I'll skin them alive. Sometimes I love you so much I feel like I could squash you into a box and just keep you under my pillow. Like a tooth.

ZAINAB. Thanks.

> *(Beat.)*

I reckon you should go home Keira –

KEIRA. Tell you what. Nearly shat myself earlier. Thought someone was at the end of my bed. Like this massive dark shape. Just towering over. Then right. Looked it dead in the eyes and realised it was me. Had my face. Spooky that.

Do you ever forget to breathe?

ZAINAB. Not really.

KEIRA. Right. I probably need to have that looked at then.

> *(Beat.)*

I've had a thought.

ZAINAB. Yeah?

KEIRA. We should climb tree before it gets too short.

ZAINAB. Eh?

KEIRA. Oaks shrink as they grow in age. So we should get up there while we can still see what's beyond.

ZAINAB. Don't think it's shrinking any time soon mate.

KEIRA. Never know. Already been here over a thousand years.

The three of us. Get to the top and howl out. That'd be magic. Don't you think?

*

> (**KEIRA'S** *stomping about swigging a bottle of red.* **ZAINAB** *and* **LUCY** *are close by the tree.)*

KEIRA Are they even allowed to do that!

LUCY. What?

ZAINAB. Block porn off the Wi-Fi.

KEIRA. That's how they control us. This school. It's mind games. They're in our minds.

> (**LUCY** *laughs.*)

Not funny.

LUCY. Sorry. Is a bit. What you gonna do?

KEIRA. I'm going to lead a protest. Going to get a railcard. Go to London. Get millions of people and armpit hair. Going to carry a big placard saying something about sexual liberation.

LUCY. Really?

KEIRA. Everything I know has fallen to shit. When am I meant to cum? Why would they do that?

ZAINAB. Dunno. To start managing expectations?

KEIRA. Managing expectations? They're meant to push us. Teach us to dream.

ZAINAB. Yeah of red-brick unis not plastic labias.

KEIRA. Even worse, you seen who we're having to draw in art?

LUCY. Don't be mean –

KEIRA. So we're told we were drawing a life model. So I'm thinking alright here we go. Then in plods this old lump. Pulls her kit off, scratches her arse and spreads her flaps for two hours. She looked like a yeti. She had one tit! And this like mental scar.

LUCY. I thought she was beautiful.

KEIRA. I thought she was a mess mate.

LUCY. Was just a bit older. That's what happens though isn't it. Should see my mum. Got a big scar round her tummy where they cut me out. Calls it her river.

ZAINAB. Biblical –

(**KEIRA** *swigs the wine.*)

KEIRA. Shitting hell. When I said bring booze Luce. Didn't mean an 18th century Malbec.

LUCY. That's all church had.

KEIRA. Takes like blood.

LUCY. Got some wafers too if you want.

KEIRA. Nah. You're alright. You want some?

ZAINAB. No thanks.

KEIRA. Suit yourself.

ZAINAB. Haven't you got a lesson next?

KEIRA. Yeah. Sex Ed. It's alright I'll just tell her I'm allergic to bananas.

ZAINAB. Nice.

KEIRA. You two are a barrel of laughs today aren't you.

LUCY. Sorry. Got a headache. All the year nines set off rape alarms, hid them in the bins. Everyone's gone mad.

KEIRA. 'Cause they've blocked a basic human right.

(**KEIRA** *takes a large swig of the wine.*)

LUCY. So loud. Had to put tampons in my ears. Like Shrek.

KEIRA. Anyone want to hang out tonight?

ZAINAB. Can't.

KEIRA. How come?

ZAINAB. Just can't.

KEIRA. Why don't you guys want to hang out with me anymore?

*(**LUCY** looks to **ZAINAB**.)*

LUCY. It's not that. Zainab's mum's not letting her hang out with us outside school.

KEIRA. Why?

LUCY. 'Cause we're girls.

ZAINAB. Was watching some...gay stuff and she walked in with a chicken kiev for me.

KEIRA. What did she say?

ZAINAB. Nothing. Just closed the door. Then when I went downstairs she wouldn't look me in the eye. Just said I'm not to be playing out with girls anymore.

KEIRA. How did you find the porn?

ZAINAB. Dunno. Softer.

> *(**LUCY** is pretending she isn't listening, but she is.)*

KEIRA. Yawn. Well. That's that then isn't it.

> *(To **LUCY**.)*

Jesus Christ's a tumble,

> *(To **ZAINAB**.)*

You're banned from your mates.

And I won't be cumming for another decade, so shall we just move to Reading, share feelings and deep-throat a shot gun?

*

> *(**LUCY** is sitting, nested by the tree. She's looking up to **KEIRA** as if she is the Messiah herself.)*

LUCY. Is it normal, you know. To be scared?

KEIRA. Scared?

LUCY. Yeah.

KEIRA. Nothing to be scared off.

LUCY. I know. But. Like you hear stories don't you. Things going wrong.

KEIRA. Blokes always know what they're doing. Just rub your nipples like this. Makes them go all hard. Like raisins.

(**LUCY** *starts rubbing her breasts.*)

And that way he knows you're enjoying it.

LUCY. ... Raisins.

Does it ever hurt?

KEIRA. Not like hurt hurt. But. Pain is just sort of what happens.

LUCY. Is it?

KEIRA. Well yeah.

LUCY. How do you stop it?

KEIRA. What?

LUCY. The hurt.

KEIRA. Well. If you focus hard enough. You can sort of separate your brain from your body.

LUCY. Really?

KEIRA. Takes practise. But. Yeah.

You just stare up above. Feel it drift off. Float away.

LUCY. That's amazing.

KEIRA. Here's one. Dig your finger nail in there.

(*She presses her nail into the flesh of her thumb.* **LUCY** *copies.*)

Yeah. That fleshy part. There. Takes the pain. Puts it somewhere else.

(**LUCY** *stays staring at her thumb.*)

LUCY. What happens if you want to be there? Like in your body.

(*Pause.*)

KEIRA. I'm proud of you mate. Honestly.

It's Eric, right?

LUCY. Haven't done anything yet.

KEIRA. Well. Just. Opening yourself up to men. It's raw. It's organic.

(*Beat.*)

LUCY. What's it like for girls?

KEIRA. What like together?

LUCY. Yeah.

KEIRA. Why –

LUCY. No reason. Just interested.

KEIRA. It's very dry. Shame Zainab's going to miss out.

LUCY. You don't get the same feelings?

KEIRA. Not with girls I'm afraid.

LUCY. You tried it?

KEIRA. Nah.

LUCY. Oh right.

KEIRA. There's nothing wrong with it. But, got to be careful what you sign up for. Just sort of nature really. Like two negative ends of a battery. They're not going to make a spark.

(**LUCY** *processes this.*)

Plus. Women are complicated. You'd know. That's why they're always axed from the bible and shit.

You good?

(*She's not.*)

LUCY. Yeah.

Okay. Last one, I swear. What happens if you want it to hurt?

(*This throws* **KEIRA**.)

KEIRA. What do you mean?

LUCY. Like. What happens if you want to feel like you're being squeezed dry by a giant fist?

(*She viscerally squishes her fist into a tight ball.* **KEIRA** *stares at her.*)

(*Then –*)

KEIRA. Fuck. It's Miss Preston. Hide.

*

(**KEIRA** *is welding a bottle of drink.* **ZAINAB** *is sitting by the tree.*)

ZAINAB. Mate

KEIRA. What?

ZAINAB. You can't just beat up a seagull.

KEIRA. Yeah I can. Doesn't belong here.

ZAINAB. So?

KEIRA. So hasn't got a right to look at me like I'm scum.

ZAINAB. I'm sure it... yeah. Alright. Whatever.

KEIRA. So I was like. Bang. BANG BANG BANG BANG BANG BANG. And it was squawking and plodding about like this...

> (**KEIRA** *stomps about imitating an aggressive seagull.*)

And I was like. You cocky little cunt. So pocketed the drugs. And went to town on it.

ZAINAB. Right.

KEIRA. Fucking deserved it.

Want some?

> (*She wiggles a tub.*)

ZAINAB. What is it?

KEIRA. Ritty.

ZAINAB. What's ritty?

KEIRA. Ritalin. Lisa's ADHD pills. You crush em up and snort them. Makes you see super clear.

ZAINAB. Won't Lisa need those?

KEIRA. Makes you see space.

ZAINAB. Won't she need them?

KEIRA. You coming out tonight? Last day of school.

ZAINAB. No.

> (**KEIRA** *kicks the tree.*)

ZAINAB. Don't do that –

> (**KEIRA** *kicks the tree again.*)

ZAINAB. Said don't –

KEIRA. Just a tree. Doesn't feel things –

ZAINAB. How do you know?

>   (**KEIRA** *looks at her, smirks to herself, backs off.*)

KEIRA.   Do you want to do things to her?

ZAINAB. Eh?

>   (**KEIRA** *starts laughing.*)

ZAINAB. What's so funny?

KEIRA. It just won't work.

Want some?

ZAINAB. You've already asked me.

KEIRA. Why her?

ZAINAB. Who?

KEIRA. Lucy. Why not me?

ZAINAB. That's not how it works.

KEIRA. Do you like her? Like proper like her?

ZAINAB. Stop taking the piss.

KEIRA. I'm not. Is it love? Like proper ugly love?

ZAINAB. She doesn't like me back.

>   (*Beat.*)

KEIRA. Oooh. That's peak. Girls. With their hashtags and
their mind games. Stay clear.

Do you fancy me?

ZAINAB. No mate.

>   (**KEIRA** *reacts like she's been shot.*)

KEIRA. Ooo. Fuck me. There's nothing worse than that.

ZAINAB. What?

(**KEIRA** *is clearly coming up on the drugs.*)

KEIRA. No one wanting to fuck you. Isn't it. There's no worse feeling than that. Oh that's cold. That's like a cold bit of meat just smacking you right in the fucking –

Found that. After I shagged Dan. Thought the nice ones might want a piece.

Turned out I was about as popular as a bomb vest in the Bullring.

Damaged goods.

I don't like fanny. Just would have been nice to be asked.

ZAINAB. I think I'm going to go –

KEIRA. Wanna try it now?

(*She grabs her own crotch.* **ZAINAB** *goes to leave.*)

KEIRA. Ah what! Only messing. Come on. I'm only playing. Just harmless playing.

(*She loops her arm over Zainab's shoulder.*)

No one likes crusty knickers and a broken heart. But that's just life isn't it. That's what happens when you go sniffing out love. You get your fingers burnt.

(*She shoots off gun fingers.*)

ZAINAB. Are you bleeding?

(**KEIRA** *studies her arm, caught for a second.*)

KEIRA. Oh yeah look at that. Think I thought I was made of pixels. So had to check.

(**ZAINAB** *frees herself from* **KEIRA**'s *embrace.*)

What? Don't look at me like that.

ZAINAB. Like what?

KEIRA. Fucking pity.

ZAINAB. Sorry.

KEIRA. Yeah don't.

ZAINAB. Since.

KEIRA. Since what.

(*They stare at each other.*)

I know you think I'm a bad person.

ZAINAB. I don't think you're a bad person.

KEIRA. I know everyone thinks I killed him.

Don't they.

*

(*August.* **LUCY** *is sitting under the tree, staring out absently. An envelope on her lap.* **ZAINAB** *enters, clutching an envelope.*)

ZAINAB. What if they're shit?

LUCY. Dunno.

ZAINAB. What happens if we don't get into sixth form?

(*Beat.*)

Will you open mine? And I'll open yours.

LUCY. Yeah alright.

(*They swap envelopes.*)

ZAINAB. I'll go behind tree.

> (*She scuttles off behind tree. After a second –*)

(Shout.) Ready?

LUCY. Ready.

> (**LUCY** *opens the envelope. Scans the letter. Beat. She smiles.* **ZAINAB** *creeps back round tree, clutching* **LUCY***'s letter.*)

Mate. You smashed it.

ZAINAB. What!

LUCY. A's and one B. A* in English Lit.

ZAINAB. No. What?

> (**ZAINAB** *grabs the envelope. Beaming.*)

Fuck.

LUCY. How did I do?

> (**ZAINAB***'s face drops.*)

What? How did I do?

> (**LUCY** *reaches out her hand.* **ZAINAB** *reluctantly offers her the letter.* **LUCY** *grabs it. She skims it.*)

> *(Beat.)*

> (**LUCY** *slowly smiles.* **ZAINAB** *breaks out into laughter.*)

ZAINAB. Fucking smashed it.

LUCY. Shit.

ZAINAB. Reckon we might actually get into uni with these.

LUCY. Like really good ones.

ZAINAB. Fuck me. I can't actually breathe.

> (**LUCY** *goes and sits down back by the tree.*
> **ZAINAB** *breathes out.*)

My mum's going to shit herself. Like properly actually shit herself. Knew we could do it Luce. If we put our minds to it. We can actually do anything. Really.

> (*Beat.*)

Wonder how everyone else has done. Wonder what Keira got? Obviously she'll have smashed it, she always gets the best marks. Wonder what Lisa Wallis has got. Hope she failed. Well. That was mean. But. Like. Hope she didn't get into sixth form. Don't you?

LUCY. I'm thinking of leaving the church.

ZAINAB. What?

LUCY. Yeah.

> (*Beat.*)

I had an orgasm.

> (*Beat.*)

ZAINAB. Woah. Isn't that –

LUCY. What?

ZAINAB. Isn't that a bit extreme? Like. Quitting your faith after a clit rub?

LUCY. It's not just that.

ZAINAB. No?

> (*Beat.*)

LUCY. I'm struggling with Him.

ZAINAB. Who?

Eric?

LUCY. No. God.

(*Beat.*)

When I had the...before I ...

ZAINAB. Yeah...

LUCY. I got the fuzzy feeling. And this like warmth.

ZAINAB. Yeah?

LUCY. And I thought of you.

(*Beat.*)

ZAINAB. Oh. Right.

LUCY. And not in a creepy way. But a –

(**ZAINAB** *kisses her.*)

ZAINAB. Sorry, I –

LUCY. Sorry. No. I just –

ZAINAB. I thought that's what you wanted.

(*Beat.*)

You don't have to look at me like that.

LUCY. Like what?

ZAINAB. Scared.

LUCY. But I am scared.

ZAINAB. Don't be scared. Just. Been wanting to.

(*Beat.*)

LUCY. How long you been sitting on that?

ZAINAB. A while.

(*Beat.*)

I … I think about you. Your dimple in your chest, you know the one, the one that can hold bath water in it.

(Pause.)

LUCY. Dig your nail in your thumb. That bit there. Takes the pain. Puts it somewhere else.

*

(The world turns. Time moves on and this is shown round the base of tree. Be it a ritual, dance, a worship, a chorus of Evangelical Christians doing the box splits – whatever. It can be absurd and gross or it can be as subtle as a leaf change. But we have to see something that connects the girls growth to the tree.)

*

(It's 2017. The girls are in year 13. Women. Whatever that means. The clunky age in-between. Still sort of half-in-their shells. But more open.)

(The tree hasn't moved. Some things just stay standing still.)

*(**KEIRA** is taking pictures of her bare feet on her phone. She's wearing home clothes. **ZAINAB** is aloud reading from 'Sapiens' by Yuval Noah Harari. She's in sixth form school uniform.)*

*(**KEIRA** changes position: lying on her back with her feet in the air.)*

*(**KEIRA** passes her a leafy twig to hold over her feet. **ZAINAB** absently holds it. Reading from the book in the other hand.)*

KEIRA. Cheers.

    (**ZAINAB** *drops the leaf.*)

Who's the writer?

ZAINAB. Yuval Noah Harari.

KEIRA. Is he single?

ZAINAB. I'm going to read a passage in assembly.

    (**KEIRA** *snorts.*)

KEIRA. Still find it crease.

ZAINAB. What?

KEIRA. You're Head Girl. They must have been on acid.

    (*She sits up. Takes another pic.*)

You got that offer then?

ZAINAB. Yeah, conditional though. Still got to get the results.

KEIRA. What was it like there?

ZAINAB. Everyone had really really really short fringes. You know the ones?

KEIRA. Trust funds and charity shop fleeces.

ZAINAB. Yeah.

KEIRA. Cunts. Got a few of those at college.

ZAINAB. Do you ever miss school?

KEIRA. Nah. Can turn up when I want now. Which, now I'm an entrepreneur, is not a fat lot.

    (**KEIRA** *passes* **ZAINAB** *the small branch again,* **ZAINAB** *holds it.*)

Right a bit.

Left a bit.

That dappled light. Yeah. Outrageous.

(*She takes a pic. Swipes on her phone screen.*)

That belongs in a fucking art gallery.

ZAINAB. Who's the bloke then?

KEIRA. Igor500.

ZAINAB. He sounds chirpy.

KEIRA. You have like a fan base. People can subscribe to see your pics. He's my best client.

ZAINAB. Client? Fuck me.

KEIRA. What?

ZAINAB. Client's a bit...

KEIRA. Bit what?

ZAINAB. Bit Amsterdam isn't it? Is he weird?

KEIRA. Can't be that weird. Got a dog in his profile pic. And he's a Wolves fan.

ZAINAB. Right. So what does he do with a pic of your feet then?

KEIRA. A finger painting. What do you think?

ZAINAB. Doesn't that make you feel...dirty?

KEIRA. Nah. It's empowering.

ZAINAB. Empowering? To have some bloke boshing one out over your toes?

KEIRA. To make money on my own terms. Yeah.

(*Beat.*)

He's hung like a gerbil. Want to see?

ZAINAB. Nah. You're alright.

(Beat.)

KEIRA. I'm exploiting a system Zainab. A system that both me and the client –

ZAINAB. Stop saying client –

KEIRA. Me and Igor500 mutually benefit from. I'm exploiting a system that exploits me.

ZAINAB. Did you hear that on a podcast?

KEIRA. Probs.

*(**KEIRA** pockets her phone.)*

At the end of the day it's forty quid for a pic of my feet. Get fifty for a nipple. Want my referral code?

ZAINAB. Nah.

KEIRA. Alright. Does Luce wanna come pub?

ZAINAB. She'll be busy.

KEIRA. Ah. Church boy. She bounced on his baritone balls yet?

*(**ZAINAB** looks at her. Shut up.)*

ZAINAB. I don't know. She doesn't tell me anything.

KEIRA. She must have done it by now.

ZAINAB. I haven't met him yet.

KEIRA. Really? I haven't either.

(Beat.)

Zainab. He eats wafers and creams over forgiveness.

She's fine.

*(**KEIRA** studies **ZAINAB**.)*

Eighteen now. Got to let sleeping dogs lie eh.

ZAINAB. What does that mean?

KEIRA. Come to think of it. Don't actually know.

*

(*The three women are by the tree.* **LUCY** *is standing, telling an animated story.* **ZAINAB** *is listening intently.* **KEIRA***, less so, is vaping.*)

LUCY. So we were watching *Blue Planet*. And what happens is these walrus climb to the top of a mountain –

KEIRA. Do walruses have legs?

LUCY. Well. No. They sort of flop to the top. And they lie there all day. On normal land. Because there's less ice. Because it's all melted. And like fifty thousand walruses needing space to breed and find fish and that. So some of these walruses have climbed –

KEIRA. Flopped –

LUCY. Flopped up this mountain. Then when it comes to home time. To get back to the ice, to their families. They have to work out how to get back down the mountain. And because their eyesight is so bad, and they can hear all these thousands of walruses on the ice below. They try and wriggle back down the mountain. But they fall.

KEIRA. Savage.

LUCY. From this huge height. Thousands and thousands of feet. They just tumble through the air. Break their backs. Break their bones. And then they just lie there. Just bodies. At the bottom of the mountain.

No questions asked.

(*Beat.*)

KEIRA. Well fuck me. Humans are beasts.

(Beat.)

ZAINAB. So Eric likes Blue Planet?

KEIRA. Ooooooh. Shade.

ZAINAB. Oh shit. No sorry. How is he?

LUCY. He's great thanks.

ZAINAB. Good.

(Beat.)

KEIRA. Is he gonna be alright skulking around here while you go uni?

*(**LUCY** shrugs.)*

LUCY. Don't know. We haven't spoken about it yet. We have the church. They'll support him.

KEIRA. When he orgasms. Does he go –

(She braces herself. Releases –)

Thelordblessyouandkeepyou.

(Beat.)

LUCY. Do you ever talk about anything other than sex?

KEIRA. Bet he's so tender in bed. Like melting butter.

*(**LUCY** shifts. **ZAINAB** goes back to her work.)*

All gracious and holy. Bet his spunk's holy water. You do have a glow to be fair.

LUCY. Thanks.

KEIRA. What do you reckon Zainab?

*(**ZAINAB** looks up, looks at **LUCY**.)*

ZAINAB. That is one spunky glow.

LUCY. Well. I really like him. He's generous. And kind.

KEIRA. He's alright.

ZAINAB. You met him?

KEIRA. Yeah. Three of us hung out week.

He saved a rabbit from the road.

(**ZAINAB** *picks at grass.*)

Got a webcam sesh tonight.

LUCY. What's in store there then?

KEIRA. The usual. Sitting on my bed. Smoking. With my baps out.

ZAINAB. Won't your dad smell it?

KEIRA. Nah. He'll be at the pub won't he.

ZAINAB. Oh yeah.

LUCY. Should be careful about that.

KEIRA. What?

LUCY. Webcam stuff. Can affect future employment can't it. Like. Once something's on camera. It's sort of just out there then isn't it.

KEIRA. Oh no.

LUCY. What?

KEIRA. You're not one of those are you?

LUCY. What?

KEIRA. Do you Blu Tack your webcam?

LUCY. Yeah?

KEIRA. Classic. I love how we think we're so important the government are actually spying through our webcams. Like no Clare from Coventry. No one actively wants to watch your flaccid nipples solidify when you bag a Tesco delivery slot.

(Beat.)

Anyway. I'm not thick. I wear a balaclava.

LUCY. Like a Ski-Chalet Barbie?

KEIRA. Like a Ski-Chalet Barbie.

ZAINAB. Now that's an image.

KEIRA. Getting one hundred for this. Soon as I hit a thousand I'm getting out of here. No questions asked. Just going to rent a flat. Just me and myself. Won't look back.

*

LUCY. You can't just do that.

ZAINAB. What?

LUCY. Not turn up?

ZAINAB. Said I'm sorry, didn't I?

LUCY. Where were you?

ZAINAB. Told you. Lost track of time.

LUCY. No one loses track of time. You're not in a Jane Austen book.

ZAINAB. I don't know what you want me to say.

LUCY. I was standing outside for an hour –

ZAINAB. I know –

LUCY. Had popcorn hidden under my jumper. Two bags. Like a pregnant woman.

ZAINAB. You've made your point –

LUCY. Had to plod home like I'd been denied an abortion –

ZAINAB. I know and I said I'm sorry.

(*Beat.*)

Thought you wouldn't care anyway.

LUCY. Why?

ZAINAB. Because you're always with him.

(*Beat.*)

LUCY. Right well that makes sense. 'Cause I made plans with *you* didn't I.

(**ZAINAB** *tries to reconnect.*)

ZAINAB. ... I slept with that girl off Hinge.

LUCY. Yeah?

ZAINAB. Yeah. Felt amazing.

LUCY. Cool.

ZAINAB. Then she said it was to 'try it out'. Said her boyfriend didn't mind.

LUCY. Right.

ZAINAB. What is that? I'm fucking eighteen and I've never felt –

LUCY. What?

ZAINAB. Loved.

LUCY. It's not all its cracked up to be.

Think it's just nice to be acknowledged isn't it.

(*Beat.*)

How are you feeling about Friday?

ZAINAB. Feel sick.

LUCY. You'll be fine.

ZAINAB. Weird isn't it. Our whole lives are hanging on an envelope.

Again.

(Beat.)

How are you feeling?

(LUCY shrugs.)

What?

LUCY. Not massively fussed.

ZAINAB. Right.

(Beat.)

LUCY. Kind of looking into options at the minute.

ZAINAB. Options?

LUCY. Just wondering if uni's what I want.

(Beat.)

ZAINAB. What? Why?

LUCY. Just 'cause.

ZAINAB. Because of what?

LUCY. Dunno. Just fancy staying here. Don't I.

ZAINAB. But you've always wanted to go to uni?

LUCY. Well. Feelings change. Sort of settled here now.

ZAINAB. Is it Eric?

LUCY. Can you stop making everything about him?

ZAINAB. Does he not want you to go?

(Beat.)

LUCY. I can make up my mind on my own you know. I am an adult.

ZAINAB. I know – just. You once thought about what was out *there* –

LUCY. Yeah and I once thought trees could talk. So...

ZAINAB. What if they can?

*

> (**ZAINAB**, **KEIRA** and **LUCY** *are standing apart, staring at an empty jam jar on the ground.*)

LUCY. I don't feel good about this.

ZAINAB. Yeah that's nasty that is.

KEIRA. Go on Lucy. Squat and cough.

LUCY. Are you sure this is legit?

KEIRA. Of course it's legit. Sending it first class.

LUCY. And you're sure Kendall Jenner does this?

KIERA. All the fucking time. Have you seen her page? Full of shit.

Quite literally.

ZAINAB. I've never seen Kendall Jenner shit in a jam jar...

KEIRA. They're all at it. These celebs.

ZAINAB. *(Getting tired of this.)* Selling bath bombs and laxative tea. Not fetish porn.

KEIRA. It's a poo. Not fetish porn. Luce will you do it? God will forgive you. Trust.

LUCY. Why can't you do it? You're the one who needs the money?

KEIRA. I can't exactly break into my old school and do a shit. And I'm not doing it on this field that would be mental. Just nip in. Please. I'll give you a cut?

LUCY. I can't mate.

ZAINAB. Don't look at me.

KEIRA. Go on.

ZAINAB. Too old for this.

KEIRA. Just 'cause you're off to uni doesn't mean you're above me.

ZAINAB. I'm not saying that.

LUCY. Forgot to say. Congrats.

ZAINAB. Thanks.

LUCY. Your first choice, right?

ZAINAB. Yeah.

LUCY. That's amazing.

> (**ZAINAB** *shoots her a brief smile.*)

ZAINAB. Have you heard yet?

> (*Beat.*)

KEIRA. (*Frantic.*) Can someone just poo in this pot please?

ZAINAB. I will personally give you thirty quid Keira.

KEIRA. Please.

ZAINAB. No.

KEIRA. Please.

ZAINAB. No.

KEIRA. Please.

ZAINAB. No –

KEIRA. FUCK SAKE.

> (**KEIRA** *explodes into tears.* **LUCY** *and* **ZAINAB** *watch her cry.*)

ZAINAB. *(Tentatively.)* Are you okay?

> (**KEIRA** *pulls herself together. Sharply.*)

KEIRA. Sorry.

Didn't sleep last night.

My dad pissed the bed.

> *(She laughs.)*

> *(She stops.)*

Think I just want to move. Now. Get out soon. You know.

Congratulations for getting into uni. That's amazing.

*

ZAINAB. WHAT?

LUCY. Doesn't matter.

ZAINAB. What is it –

> *(Breath.)*

LUCY. Eric has asked me to marry him.

> *(Beat.)*

ZAINAB. No he hasn't.

LUCY. What?

ZAINAB. You're eighteen?

LUCY. So?

ZAINAB. So that's mental. What have you said?

What have you said?

LUCY. Said I'd think about it. Need a few days to. Let it all go round my head.

>   (*Beat.*)

He's a good person Zainab. He's had a really rough time of it. But he's good. And he's kind. He's so so kind. It's weird. I feel like a child again. Looked after. Haven't had that since I was a kid. I know it's not the same but.

>   (*Pause.*)

ZAINAB. Okay

>   (*Pause.*)

What happened to your arm?

LUCY. My arm?

ZAINAB. Yeah. There.

>   (*She points to Lucy's wrist.*)

By your wrist. Underneath.

>   (**LUCY** *looks, then matter of fact –*)

LUCY. Oh. It's a bruise.

ZAINAB. What from?

>   (*There's a silent stand off between them.*)

LUCY. A thing we do.

ZAINAB. A thing?

LUCY. Like a game.

ZAINAB. A game?

LUCY. Yeah. He lies on the bed and…and I kneel there.

ZAINAB. Bit of a strange game. Who won that time?

LUCY. What are you on about?

ZAINAB. Why have you got marks round your wrist?

LUCY. Because I'm tied up.

(*Beat.*)

ZAINAB. With what?

LUCY. Sometimes a belt or rope or whatever.

ZAINAB. Why?

LUCY. Why what?

ZAINAB. Why do you let him?

LUCY. Let him? I want him to.

You don't give a shit when Keira's bleeding all over the tennis court.

(*Beat.*)

It doesn't hurt.

ZAINAB. Why have you got bruises then?

LUCY. Because I bruise like a peach. Remember, when I fell out of tree? That night we climbed it. You had to carry me home.

(*Beat.*)

ZAINAB. So he's a sadist –

LUCY. He's my fiancé.

ZAINAB. You haven't said yes yet.

LUCY. I intend to.

I'm really sorry if that's hard for you. I am. I just wish you'd give him a chance.

(*Beat.*)

Can't you?

ZAINAB. No. Sorry.

>   (**LUCY** *shrugs.*)

LUCY. I'm really sorry I don't know what to say to that.

ZAINAB. You upset?

LUCY. Well. A bit.

>   (*Beat.*)

ZAINAB. Can I hug you?

>   (*Beat.*)

LUCY. I don't think that's a good idea.

>   *

>   (**KEIRA** *and* **ZAINAB** *are sitting, staring out at the dark field, soggy bottoms.*)

KEIRA. So she said yes?

ZAINAB. Yep.

KEIRA. That'll be fun won't it. Always fancied myself at a wedding. White flowers in my hair. Wonder how old the priest is. Reckon she'll have me as a bridesmaid? It would be clapped wouldn't it, if she didn't make us bridesmaids?

ZAINAB. Yeah. I don't know.

KEIRA. Cheer up mate. Will be cool to be in a church. Hope I don't burst into flames. That would be a bit dry. Imagine that. Lucy gliding down the aisle and I'm just blazing up like Guy Fawkes at the back. You been to her church?

ZAINAB. Yeah. Dan's funeral.

>   (**KEIRA** *shifts.*)

Not been in one since.

KEIRA. Want one of these?

ZAINAB. What is it?

KEIRA. Like an opioid. Bit less bait.

ZAINAB. I'm not taking heroin.

KEIRA. Fuck me. We're not about to strap up and kill a
baby. Just a nice little buzz.

>   *(Beat.)*

They take pain away.

>   (**ZAINAB** *looks at Keira's outstretched palm.*)

ZAINAB. Yeah alright.

>   (**ZAINAB** *picks it up.* **KEIRA** *swallows hers.*
>   **ZAINAB** *stares at the pill in her palm.*)

KEIRA. Give it five. We'll be in space.

>   *(The girls both sit there, staring out ahead.)*

Do you still love her then?

ZAINAB. Just a bit.

KEIRA. I'm sorry about that.

ZAINAB. Not your fault.

KEIRA. Is a bit though isn't it?

>   *(Beat.)*

You gonna have that?

ZAINAB. Nah.

>   (*She passes it back.* **KEIRA** *smiles at the*
>   *familiarity. Worth a shot.*)

>   (*She looks up at the sky.*)

KEIRA. Bumped into Lisa Wallis the other day.

ZAINAB. Oh right.

KEIRA. She was in Co-Op.

ZAINAB. How was that?

KEIRA. Was grand. She's got a baby.

ZAINAB. Not surprised.

KEIRA. Ah. I don't know. Don't think that's fair. People's life choices and that.

ZAINAB. Yeah. People's life choices. She told the whole school I was going to grope them in their sleep.

KEIRA. That's just kids though isn't it.

> *(Beat.)*

The more we grow the more I feel like I'm shrinking. Shrinking so small I just disappear. Sometimes imagine the world without me in it.

ZAINAB. Don't say that.

KEIRA. No. I don't mean. Just. Always thought I'd be something. But life just always seems to get in the way doesn't it. Feel old. Tired.

> *(Beat.)*

Sometimes wonder if that's how Dan felt.

I wonder if he thought of me. Like if I was the last image in his mind. Wonder if he hated me. Maybe I hate me too.

KEIRA. God my breath feels.

> *(Beat.)*

ZAINAB. We fucked up there mate. It wasn't your fault.

KEIRA. What?

ZAINAB. Yeah. It was never your fault Keira.

(**KEIRA** *looks to* **ZAINAB**.)

KEIRA. Really?

(*Pause.*)

Oh. Okay.

Bit confusing all that stuff isn't it.

That's weird. My heart just feels. Lighter. Think I was carrying that. Somewhere in my body.

(*She wriggles her neck.*)

But I don't want to be a victim. No one wants that. The biographies and the shiny make-up. Don't want a fucking statue.

ZAINAB. I won't make a statue of you. Don't worry.

KEIRA. Want to be remembered for something great. Not for being…

Fuck me. This pill is.

Remember when we climbed tree? The three of us. Before Lucy fell out of it. Remember how we felt the world turning.

(**KEIRA** *stares at* **ZAINAB**.)

I saw her look at you. And I was so jealous. I couldn't ever imagine being looked at like that. She had the whole view above the clouds. Was hanging on the edge of something. And she looked back down. She had all the world to look at. And she chose to look at you.

(*Pause.*)

What time's your train?

ZAINAB. Seven.

KEIRA. Not long now.

ZAINAB. Not long now.

KEIRA. That'll be good won't it. Getting out.

ZAINAB. You are too. Saved up enough haven't you.

(**KEIRA** *takes a massive swig of her drink.*)

KEIRA. Nah. That's not happening anymore.

ZAINAB. Eh?

KEIRA. I don't have the money anymore.

ZAINAB. Why not?

KEIRA. Dad spent it.

ZAINAB. What?

KEIRA. Yeah.

ZAINAB. What's he spent it on?

KEIRA. Have a guess.

(**ZAINAB** *goes to speak –*)

Don't make a scene. Can't be arsed.

(*Beat.*)

You'd best get a move on.

ZAINAB. I can't just leave you –

KEIRA. Go on. Piss off. I'll be seeing you soon.

You've got to go now mate. Go and see what's beyond.

(*She stands, wobbles about a bit.*)

IN THE GREAT UNKNOWN.

ZAINAB. But mate –

KEIRA. Go on. [You're going to be late for your train.]

(Same time as **LUCY** *below.)*

(Time overlaps. **KEIRA***'s gone.)*

LUCY. [You're going to be late for your train.]

(Beat.)

So what? We just stand here?

ZAINAB. Yeah. I'm not going anywhere.

LUCY. That's ridiculous –

ZAINAB. I don't care.

(Beat.)

LUCY. What do you want from me?

ZAINAB. I want you to go to university.

LUCY. Oh my God Zainab. Drop it.

ZAINAB. Once I leave this town Luce. I'm not coming back. I swear. I'm gone. I'm not looking back.

(Beat.)

So you either come with me or –

LUCY. Don't give me an ultimatum –

ZAINAB. Don't make me have to.

LUCY. Why do you have to do this?

ZAINAB. What?

LUCY. Piss everything up for me?

ZAINAB. Because I'm tired of you being a pussy flap Luce –

LUCY. Stop talking like that –

ZAINAB. Sorry –

LUCY. So what? I come with you. Then what?

ZAINAB. I know it's insane but we can work it out.

LUCY. I –

ZAINAB. Just come with me –

LUCY. Why?

ZAINAB. Just because –

LUCY. Piss off.

ZAINAB. I love you.

> *(Beat.)*

LUCY. You love me?

ZAINAB. Yeah.

> *(Beat.)*

Would you like me to give you the logical explanation as to why you need to come with me –

LUCY. There's no logic to it –

ZAINAB. Why?

LUCY. I can't even get the train. It's in ten minutes.

ZAINAB. Right. Well. Fuck the timings. I'll get the next one. With you.

> *(**LUCY** raises her eyebrows.)*

LUCY. Go on then.

ZAINAB. What?

LUCY. The logical explanation –

ZAINAB. Right. Yes. I've been thinking about the network of how all this works.

LUCY. How what works?

ZAINAB. How I think me and you operate –

LUCY. Right. Go on.

ZAINAB. I've been thinking about systems.

    Political anatomy

    Social hierarchy

    Power structures

    How they're designed to divide

    To control

    Been thinking about how I'd dismantle them

    Have a mild panic attack then think about how I'd put them back together –

LUCY. What are you even saying –

ZAINAB. What I'm trying to say. Is the Virgin Mary didn't have an intact hymen Lucy.

    It's bollocks.

    How are we supposed to fit into a structure if it's built on fucking lies?

    It's ridiculous. It's designed to stop us. To suffocate us.

    (Beat.)

    Or maybe I'm insane.

    Maybe it's all in our minds.

    And it was fear that kept us apart. That time. When we were kids.

    Three girls who couldn't bear to dream of bliss because it would have been too painful if we never reached it.

    (Beat.)

    I want to love you.

    I want you to let me love you.

I'd never hurt you.

I promise.

I'd be gentle with you.

I'd let you be strong.

And if ever I made you feel small I'd want you to slap me.

And I'd never do it again.

Because I see us Luce

I honestly do.

Reading on a beach

Combing nits out our kids hair

Bitching about the greasy psycho who gave them to her

Fucking up

And whatever is up there, whoever it is. If it's God with his hands down his pants, or some weird physicist holding the stars like they're sticks in the playground

Who ever it is I want them to look down on us and think

Fuck

That's it. That. Is. It. Those two. I did it.

And it's fucking beautiful.

> *(Beat.)*

So if I wait here. Like a dickhead. Right by tree. And you go home, pack your stuff. We'll get on that train.

Together. Yeah?

> *(**LUCY** looks down at her shifting feet.)*

> *(Pause.)*

Please can you just –

LUCY. Okay.

I'll come.

Fuck it.

Wait here.

> *(They stare at each other. A millions shards of whatever time and space is, passing between them.)*

> *(**LUCY** goes.)*

ZAINAB. I'll stay here.

I'll be here.

Swear down I'll be here.

> *(**KEIRA** enters.)*

KEIRA. What are you still doing here?

ZAINAB. What?

KEIRA. I thought you were off to uni.

ZAINAB. I am.

KEIRA. Why are you still here?

ZAINAB. I was just –

KEIRA. You alright?

ZAINAB. Yeah, yeah. I'm sorry. I'm –

> *(There's a crack in Zainab's memory. The world turns. **LUCY** enters.)*

LUCY. Do you want to hear my poem?

Tree by Lucy.

There's a Tree. It's as old as time.

Been here for plenty long.

Seen it all, time and time again,

Awakening from its slumber.

ZAINAB. Lucy are you –

LUCY. The tree stirs –

ZAINAB. What are you doing?

LUCY. Its roots bury deeper and thicker into the earth, churning up rabbits and squirrels and flinging them up into the sky. Thud thud thud –

ZAINAB. What are you doing?

> *(An ear-splitting sound. Time is moving. The world is turning.)*

ZAINAB. Fuck.

My head.

Jesus

That –

Can you hear that?

KEIRA. The tree stirs and Anne Boleyn mourns on the soil of her successors. Then her head snaps off and flies off up into the sky.

ZAINAB. Wait. Fuck. Tree? How long have I been here? Something's moving.

LUCY. The tree stirs and all the bracken and broken dreams crawl out from underground and cut your cheeks and drag your hair.

> *(The world turns. **ZAINAB** crouches down holding her ears. The sound is horrible.)*

ZAINAB. Tree. Can you hear me are you listening?

KEIRA. The world turns and you might write a poem about it but it keeps turning so you close your eyes instead.

ZAINAB. Tree. Please just fucking. Talk to me. Tell me.

LUCY. The world turns and a flash of you and I rips the sky in two and time freezes...

Just for a fraction of a second.

(**ZAINAB** and **LUCY** look at each other.)

LUCY. Before it continues its inevitable revolve...

(*The world turns and snaps and drops down to its back legs and crawls.*)

KEIRA & LUCY. And Eve and all the women who have been before roar louder than ever then laugh at the predestined fate that it is far from over as time repeats itself again and again and again and again and again and again and again and again and again and again and again and again and again and again and again again and again and again and again and again and again again and again again and again and again and again and again and again again and again again and again and again and again again again and again again and again and again and again and again and again and again again and again and again and again...

(**KEIRA** binds Lucy's wrists. They grip each other. Lean back. Wedding confetti.)

(*Light radiates down as* **ZAINAB** *reads the final section. Its peace and inevitability. Bells. Orchestral.*)

ZAINAB. And when light finally seeps back in, the tree sighs. It's felt women pass around its base time and time again. And it thinks, oh no here we go again.

(**LUCY** *smiles up at the final light. And then it dies.*)

*

(**ZAINAB** *is sitting silently by tree. She looks like a child slumped in a heap at its base. But she's now twenty four. It's 2024, time's moved on again.*)

(*Enter* **KEIRA**. **ZAINAB** *looks up at her, like she's a ghost. After a sec –*)

KEIRA. Hi.

(*Pause.*)

We had the same idea then.

(*Nothing.* **KEIRA** *nods, she looks up at the tree.*)

Tree's changed.

ZAINAB. Has it?

(**KEIRA** *looks at it again, contemplates.*)

KEIRA. Uh. No. Don't know why I said that.

(*Pause.*)

Do you want a custard cream? They got a bit fucked in my pocket but...

ZAINAB. No. Thank you.

(*Pause.*)

KEIRA. You look...well.

ZAINAB. You too.

(*Pause.*)

KEIRA. How was uni?

ZAINAB. Good.

KEIRA. Are you working?

ZAINAB. I was.

>   *(Beat.)*

KEIRA. I'm up in the Lake District. Work at Beatrix Potter's house.

>   *(Beat.)*

Yeah. Had to dress up as a fuck-off sized puddle duck on my first day. Plod about giving tours. Now I just read stories to the kiddies and stuff.

>   *(Beat.)*

ZAINAB. Why the Lake District?

KEIRA. It's peaceful. Feels like you're trapped in the past.

>   *(Beat.)*

Finally got that railcard. Hit twenty four and thought. Hang on. Got to get a move on with that. Nearly twenty five and then it's all over.

ZAINAB. … I think there's a twenty-five to thirty one now.

KEIRA. You're joking.

>   (**ZAINAB** *nods.*)

Right. Well. Good to know.

>   *(She looks up at the branches again. Silence.)*

It's been a minute. Been what?

ZAINAB. Six years.

KEIRA. Yeah. Well.

I mean, I saw you at the…

(*Pause.*)

Sent you a message when... Did you get it?

Because it said you'd read it. And. No stress but.

(*Beat.*)

ZAINAB. Sorry, I wasn't expecting to see you today.

KEIRA. Yeah. I know I haven't been...

(*Beat.*)

Where were you, when you found out?

ZAINAB. Tesco Express.

Where were you?

KEIRA. I was at home. Stood in the back garden and looked out down at the forest. Felt like I stood there for days.

(*Pause.*)

When will we find out?

ZAINAB. Anytime now. Lucy's mum said she'll call.

KEIRA. Fuck.

(*Beat.*)

Do you reckon there's a chance it was?

ZAINAB. What?

KEIRA. An accident.

(**ZAINAB** *stiffens.*)

Sorry I didn't mean –

ZAINAB. You. There. Saying that.

KEIRA. I was just wondering –

ZAINAB. You just turned back into a kid.

KEIRA. What?

ZAINAB. She was a child.

KEIRA. She was twenty three.

>   *(Beat.)*

ZAINAB. Why haven't you been at the trial?

>   *(Beat.)*

KEIRA. Didn't want to see her being...picked apart on a powerpoint.

ZAINAB. Right.

>   *(Beat.)*

KEIRA. What?

>   *(Beat.)*

ZAINAB. If you hadn't been so.

KEIRA. What?

ZAINAB. Nothing.

KEIRA. No go on. Say it.

>   *(Beat.)*

ZAINAB. She learnt...that from someone.

KEIRA. And you think that person was me.

>   *(**KEIRA** stares at her.)*

She told me you just stopped replying to her one day. You just disappeared.

ZAINAB. I was at uni.

KEIRA. No it wasn't that. You were proud. She didn't come back to tree that night, before your train.

ZAINAB. She married him.

KEIRA. And that meant losing you as a friend did it?

(*Beat.*)

ZAINAB. She didn't want me around, he'd convinced her of that.

(*Beat.*)

KEIRA. I know it suits you, the idea that the rest of us are suffering and you're the fixed mark. Standing still. I know how you watched me. That I was a kid who didn't know better. But I was alright. I was having a bad time with my dad and yeah I got a bit carried away sometimes. But pitying me suited you. It gave you power. To rule over me, to judge.

And I think it gave you power over Lucy. But you aren't a saviour Zainab. You let her down.

ZAINAB. Are you saying it's my fault?

KEIRA. No. I'm saying that maybe she was happy. With him.

(*Beat.*)

Has it ever occurred to you that Lucy...wanted it? That maybe saying she was forced isn't...right.

(*Beat.*)

I have dreams about ripping his fucking eyeballs out every night. But I just can't forget that – she wanted to feel...and I'm sorry that that has lead to...

ZAINAB. So you're saying she asked for it?

KEIRA. I'm just saying that maybe it was a game that went wrong.

(*Beat.*)

(**ZAINAB** *stares cold at her.*)

ZAINAB. You know a human body can be without oxygen
for four to six minutes. Permanent brain damage
comes after four usually death at around six. That's if
your thyroid hasn't been snapped before.

The autopsy showed he strangled her for eight minutes.
So she was probably dead for two minutes before he
stopped.

Are you telling me she wanted that?

That she consented to her own murder?

KEIRA. I don't know –

ZAINAB. They were showing blood circulation graphs –

KEIRA. Zainab.

ZAINAB. They held her fucking pants up –

KEIRA. Stop.

ZAINAB. You should be ashamed.

KEIRA. Oh I am.

I feel so much shame I sometimes think of clogging
myself up so nothing is ever born into this shame again.

But I'm tired. I don't want to do it anymore. Round
these roots.

I don't want to believe that he did that...deliberately...

Because that would mean he meant to hurt my friend.

So I'm sorry. I won't.

ZAINAB. Why?

KEIRA. Because I can't carry that pain too.

(*Pause.*)

Who's telling them to do this to us?

Who's to blame Zainab?

Who is it who –

It can't be those stupid beautiful boys in the playground, can it? Can't be them. 'Cause they're just as new as we were.

(Beat.)

Is it just written in the stars?

Is it in our fingertips when we're born?

Who decides that?

When was that decided?

> (**ZAINAB** *looks up at tree for a while.*)

ZAINAB. I didn't go for the verdict today because she once told me if I didn't believe in God. I could believe in tree. She said it knows all the answers.

KEIRA. Maybe it does.

> (**KEIRA** *sits at the base of the tree. Leans her head back. Dappled light coming through the leaves.*)

KEIRA. God that's bliss isn't it.

> (**ZAINAB** *sits next to her, leans her head back.*)

ZAINAB. Been thinking about time. Filling in the gaps in time, in my head. Putting them all back together. Moments of us round here.

> (**KEIRA** *smiles.*)

> *(Silence.)*

KEIRA. Could you imagine if they never came back. If they were like right, fuck this, let's hit Mexico. They're like beeping through customs right now. With condoms and Toblerones. And we're just waiting here forever. Just rinsing church Malbec and talking about our feelings.

>   (**ZAINAB** *kind of laughs.*)

ZAINAB. Why are you like this?

KEIRA. Because if I wasn't I'd cry.

Forever.

And I wouldn't stop.

And I'm not gonna do that.

So we're going to keep moving. We won't ever –

>   *

>   (**LUCY** *sprints into the space. She's fifteen, getting a leg up from* **KEIRA**.)

LUCY. STOP!!!!!!!!!!!!

KEIRA. What?!

LUCY. Snapping at my heels –

KEIRA. *(Sarcasm.)* Well take your time.

LUCY. Alright. Give us a sec.

>   (**ZAINAB** *pulls her eyes from the dappled leaves. She looks at her friends.*)

KEIRA. Fuck me. Don't look up that skirt.

ZAINAB. Eh?

KEIRA. Found that squirrels family.

LUCY. What?

KEIRA. Never mind.

ZAINAB. Don't be gross.

KEIRA. Fuck me it's freezing.

ZAINAB. No clouds.

> (**ZAINAB** *calls up.*)

You up yet?

LUCY. What?

ZAINAB. Said you up yet?

LUCY. Woah!

ZAINAB. What is it?

> (**LUCY** *howls into the sky.*)

LUCY. Can see roof tops! Can see the world turning!

KEIRA. Can you?

LUCY. Yeah! Get up here!

ZAINAB. I'm going to leave this one. Too high!

LUCY. But you have to! See what's beyond!

KEIRA. Fuck it. I'm going up. Give us a leg up.

> (**ZAINAB** *gives* **KEIRA** *a leg up.*)

ZAINAB. Go on.

KEIRA. Can you see the planets mate?

LUCY. Past the planets!

KEIRA. Woah! Wait for us!

> (**LUCY** *howls out again.* **KEIRA** *climbs up.*)

> (**ZAINAB** *looks up.*)

> (**LUCY** *drops her head down, turns to face* **ZAINAB**.)

LUCY. You coming?

You're missing the view.

ZAINAB. Nah. I'm not.

> (**ZAINAB** *looks up at her. She smiles.* **KEIRA** *yells from the top of the tree.*)

KEIRA. Come on!

ZAINAB. Alright!

I'm coming.

KEIRA. Can see the world turning!

LUCY. Come on then.

ZAINAB. I'm coming up.

I'm coming.

> (*They start the climb.*)

*